More praise for Steve Brightman:

"In 1931, the Cleveland Indians were kicked out of League Park into the larger, wider Cleveland Stadium, much as Adam and Eve had been kicked out of Eden and left to roam the world. Steve Brightman takes the original power couple and transplants them into a city so modern it may as well be timeless (indeed, he explicitly tells us that "Past, present, and future are all visible at once." [--'serpent announces the final birth of adam']). Adam pogoes us from Genesis to Revelation, with every conceivable stop in between, Eve breaking in like Nancy Sinatra in "Some Velvet Morning" once in a while to sing to seven and a half billion Cains and Abels of a future that wants to be a present. Adam embraced the confluence of architecture and munitions in 1951; League Park was, for the most part, razed. But Adam is stubborn enough to "...refuse[...] to admit/every heartbeat is a jailbreak" [--'adam loops experimental art on his living room wall'], and thus here we are, with a pretty darn magnificent collection in front of us."

- Robert Beveridge

"In this dense metamodern reimagination of the Adam and Eve mythology, Steve Brightman wrestles artfully with what it means to be a white man in today's world with authenticity, inventiveness, wit, and deep intelligence."

- Michelle Smith Quarles

Other works by Steve Brightman:

Leaving the Flatlands to the Amateurs
(Alien Buddha Press 2020)

History, Too, Is A Simple Machine
(NightBallet Press 2015)

*The Wild Gospel of Careening and Other Sermons
from the Rumble Strip*
(Red Orchid Publishing 2015)

13 Ways of Looking at Lou Reed
(Crisis Chronicles Press 2013)

Like Michelangelo Sorta Said
(Poet's Haven Press 2013)

In Brilliant Explosions Alone
(NightBallet Press 2013)

Absent The
(Writing Knights Press 2013)

Sometimes, Illinois
(NightBallet Press 2012)

The Logic of Meteors
(Writing Knights Press 2011)

Forlorn Teeth
(Blasted Press 2011)

THE CIRCUS OF HIS BONES

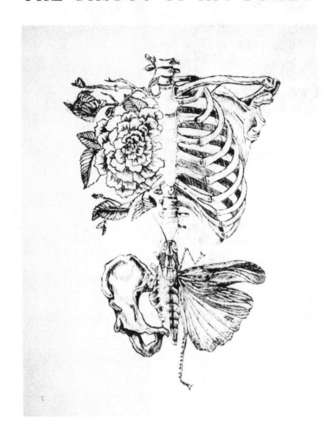

Poems by Steve Brightman

Kung Fu Treachery Press

Rancho Cucamonga, CA

Copyright © Steve Brightman, 2020

First Edition: 1 3 5 7 9 10 8 6 4 2

ISBN: 978-1-952411-34-2

LCCN: 2020948411

Cover: the art of Matt Miller

Author photos: Theresa Göttl Brightman

Acknowledgments:

Thank you to every person who has offered me their time, their words, or their laughter; all of which, we've learned this year, are such valuable commodities. Thank you to Jason Ryberg for giving me the space to birth this collection and then put it into our world. Thank you to Colum McCann for changing the way I read the written word. Thank you to Joe Henry for verbalizing all of our mortality by facing his own so openly.

Table of Contents

THE CIRCUS OF HIS BONES

For Theresa, my first set of eyes and
my daily reminder to hope.

It gets to seem as if way back in the Garden of Eden after the Fall, Adam and Eve had begged the Lord to forgive them and He, in his boundless exasperation had said, "All right, then. Stay. Stay in the Garden. Get civilized. Procreate. Muck it up." And they did.

-Diane Arbus

serpent announces the first birth of adam

All good myths begin with a bird or a human
far too curious or callous and sometimes mistaken

by a distracted and careless manner of youth,
well before they realize the expense of free.

Past, present, and future are all visible at once.
Once upon a time plus once upon a midnight dreary

plus once upon a dream plus once upon a child.
This is the adding machine where adam was born.

adam names the birds that have already
been named

Yell streaks
down to him
from streetlight.
In a blackened
consequence,
he yells back;
strains his vocal
chords, knowing
he has mangled
his first attempt;
coughs to clear
his mouth of
misconstructed
vowels and says
"crow" again.

adam reads from darwin 3:16

Beloved, we know
how our vestigial tails
sometimes cause us
to squirm in our chairs,
or how our fight or flight
instincts opened valleys
of doubt under the clouds.

Brothers and sisters,
we understand in the
deepened marrow
of our earthly bones
the blessed unruliness of
our unseemly body hair,
and the embarrassment of
our mammalian impulses.

adam learns three basic truths

He cannot bullshit children or dogs.
He can try, but eventually honesty
will be the thing he has forgotten.
It is the only thing they can hear.

Light might be the best disinfectant
for ridding himself of vermin,
but light also shines the brightest
on his flaws – he knows the ones,
the ones he always see best in others.

When the mountain is hunting him,
it is not in any hurry to find him. It
knows where he sleeps and moves
him closer to the avalanche tonight.

eve sings to their offspring, song one

daughters and sons
the voice of your mother/was the first voice you knew/
summer turning into fall/is the beta version of your bones
decaying/dress for the occasion/leaves are shiny on one
side and/the other side is built for thirst/tomorrow may
be the last full day/without another headstone in your
life/take full advantage of easy breathing and/your soft
comfortable middle/absent any hunger pains/desire can
rot you from the inside out and/you will not see any
bruising/until well after it is too late

adam realizes the mistake in trusting the worst
gut instinct ever

In the not so distant past,
adam didn't much bother
with whether or not the bubble
was centered. He figured
if it looked level, it must be level.
He had convinced himself
                    that he could cleave himself
from the sins of the world by sight,
by sound, or by avoidance.
He had convinced himself
that he was the only arbiter
and the only impetus in
moving his forsaken skin.

adam stencils his name into the sun, more or less

In his spare time, he pours
the yellow slope of sun into whatever
containers he can find that day.
He never knows when he might need light.
This Thursday past, he ladled liquid gold
in small but equal portions into a
dozen dozen dusty cups and mugs.
Each of them had a-d-a-m stenciled
in black across their flat bottoms.
That's one hundred and forty-four times
for those of you who are rusty with
the mathematics. That's one hundred
and forty-four times his name was staring
him in his face, swelling his tongue with
confusion and a pair of belligerent consonants.

adam loops experimental art upon his
living room wall

but he disregards
the perimeter con job.
Every wall is not
a load-bearing wall.

adam knocks them down,
ignoring any repercussions
regarding structure.
He tilts color on its side
and sets it to bake
under the refractor sun.

He counts every number
in every head as if they
are in a silent conspiracy
against themselves.
He is still figuring out
that every ulna is a crowbar.
He refuses to admit
every heartbeat is a jailbreak.

eve sings to their offspring, song two

daughters and sons
keep both eyes open for intersections/see them for what
they are/yellow lights are a caution/only while you are
driving/the sun is a yellow dwarf/while you are sitting
here breathing and/some dead folks are dead folks/
because someone/couldn't see anything but red

adam takes deep cleansing breaths
without doing yoga

He pinpoints a mark
in the shadow of his scapula,
presses his thumb there,
on the nights that he is
flexible enough to do so.
He applies pressure until
his empty lungs thrust forward
into new air or until the pain
is so great that he sympathizes
with the angels who left the earth
of their own free will. He holds
his breath and counts to ten.
He exhales.

adam introduces himself to winter

February beat down
on adam's
nearly nude body.
It wasn't exactly
enlightenment
that he felt
when he fell
through a hole
in the ice.
It was more release,
than anything.
He closed his eyes
and blindly floated
through a growing
white rumble of
spectacle and nerves,
leaving his lungs
to expand and contract
underneath a blurred
and awkward sun.

adam finds himself the unwitting subject of the first book of osteology

There were days,
back when reagan was king,
when adam was angry
at every one of
his 206 bones.
His skin was ready to quit,
and he had somehow managed
to convince his organs
that they would be better off
if they gave up, too.

His bones, though,
they were stubborn.

They were invested
in keeping him upright.
His bones, though,
they were right.
They were invested
in keeping him
stubborn.

eve sings to their offspring, song three

daughters and sons
the shelf life of magic/decreases exponentially in
sunlight/do not fall in love with the iron and electricity/
in your own blood/science is reckless with the human
heart/math too has abandoned anything resembling
organs or bones/your spine can keep you upright/only
until you notice that it is doing so

adam opens a library

One became two
became not three,

but twelve. Rivers
became mathematics.

Churches stayed churches,
but opened their arms

to the idea of every book
being the good book.

Love was less bludgeon
than default response.

adam writes a billy collins poem

"It was hot that day. It's always hotter in your memory.
It was hot that day and I think we had lemonade.

We paid ten bucks to park and walk around downtown.
The art museum closed early that day -

oh yeah, it must have been a Sunday that day -
so there was nothing to do but watch the locals.

I think I bought a lemonade, because a lemonade
would be nice in memory and I just realized this poem

is starting to sound more like a billy collins poem
than an actual memory, so scratch the fucking lemonade."

adam instinctively loses concern
for the axis of why

It started deep
within his genetics
in places that
weren't named yet.
In places where
ideas began
at the most
elemental level
and in places
where predators
thrive on the dark
and tentative irons
in the blood.
Night is coming
earlier now and adam
doesn't understand
the axis of why,
he only knows
that he is hungry
and you are close.

serpent announces the second birth of adam

Feathered things escape upon air faster than an eyeblink.
Forestry is good for cover, but only until nightfall.

All good myths begin with a bird or a human,
but darkness brings a different predator.

Rugged foliage serves as his swaddling clothes.
The scruff of his neck still has loose enough skin

for carrying, one clenched jaw from the Donner Party.
This is the food chain where adam was born.

adam embraces the confluence of
architecture and munitions

Gravity is easy from the inside.

A well-placed detonation
and the structure
collapses into the shadow
of its own footprint.

Gravity is brutal from the inside.

A well-placed word from
the wrong damn mouth,
a well-timed look from
the wrong damn face and
a strong spine crumbles.

adam tiptoes through the night, to no avail

Three long floorboards
in the bedroom creak

with a different set
of urgencies beneath

adam's shuffling feet than
they do beneath hers.

adam unfolds the immediate

adam spent most of his day
running yellow lights,
watching them unnaturally
bloom in the winter sun.
It was a stunning display,
this seemingly endless traffic bouquet
unfolding in the immediate
blue above him; like the scene
in any heist movie where all the pins
align perfectly inside the lock and
a studio-engineered click
echoes so loudly that the sinner
freezes for a split-second.

eve sings to their offspring, song four

daughters and sons
the sun and the air are liars/warm is as much a religion
as an insurgency is/hastily scribbled on the nearest piece
of anything/which resembles a flat surface/this does not
make anger a house of worship/your body is a temple/
your neighbor's body is a temple, too

adam battles electronica

He lives for
the brilliant
simplicities
of the apple,
the aviary,
the apostle,
the acorn.

No installation,
no devices,
no software
required.

He lives sky,
soap, song.
He lives stone.
He lives stars.

No diagnostics,
no product key,
no setting of
preferences.

adam reflects upon what he used to be

Tree was a ladder
before daddy took

a turn as an angry
magician, counting

off his closed-fist
abracadabras before

disappearing in a
cloud of red dust.

Tree was a ladder
so that adam could

look down upon
morning glories,

blue innocence then,
and still a north star.

adam succumbs to his shyness and refuses
to join the chorus

adam saw her
left hand was
a fistful of locusts,
her right was drawn
into a fist except
her curled index finger,
tracing the perforation
between sun and earth.
The oceans and horizon
were a choir singing along
with her every move -
deepest voices were the
angels, with the sinners
in falsetto harmony.

eve sings to their offspring, song five

daughters and sons
say your hellos goodbyes to each other/remind yourselves/
that the desert is a desert for a reason/there is no need to walk
through it just because it is there/remind yourselves/that the
ocean is an ocean for a reason/don't expect your friends to
meet you every time you come up for air/some days you have
to swim for your lives/and it's hard damn work/remembering
which body of blue/is sky and which is water

adam calculates the distance between
glass and light

Iron & gold are
the only metals older,
but neither of them
glint the Chilean sky
the way that copper does
but neither of them
keep the condor's eye
the way that copper does.
Every corrosive shade
of green and blue
dance on the head of a pin
like a beautiful battalion
of brushstrokes, like every
emergency room should
close their sliding glass doors.
The fallen angels,
the bloodied angels,
the bruised and weary angels
ache from arching
their shoulders upward,
ache from trying to keep
electrochemical wings
from dragging behind them
in the sour blue-green blend
between southern Andes
and lower heavens.

adam patiently wraps his tongue around that
wretched negative

One N.
One O.

All No.

Tonight, he patiently envies its efficiency,
its sledgehammer singular syllable.
Tonight, he patiently envies that wretched negative.
Tonight, No breathes easy.

It has earned the penthouse suite.
it has earned the extra fifteen minutes in the hot tub.
There will be turn-down service.
No has earned the comfort of sleep.
It will kick its feet up and enjoy the
complimentary starbucks in the morning.

No will grow complacent. No is young.
No doesn't yet know that this is a long fight.
No doesn't yet know that a bloodied nose
is not a submission.

adam marvels at feats of engineering prowess

And just like that,
red clay disaster
was averted. adam
watched her hold
back the sun,
readjust light
to a more usable
temperature,
wield mortar
and trowel like
they were the last
weapons forged
for mankind, and
rebuild the hearth
from inside their
crumbling walls.

eve sings to their offspring, song six

daughters and sons
don't confuse your medicine with your healing/your skin
doesn't have to be/a small cacophony of demons/expose
yourself to natural light and remember that/the mythology
behind everything/probably came from the voice of a man/
who was angry at the gods/because his power was not as vast
as he hoped

adam stumbles through an odd but necessary
lesson on courtship

Through a series
of trial and error,
(mostly error,
if we are being honest
with each other)
adam has reached
the conclusion
that despite a fine mist
and a healthy amount of
greenery behind him,
he cannot just walk up to
a woman, no matter
how well he thinks
he knows her,
and hand her
organic produce.

adam remembers the stars

Every flat space is a bed
every open field is a
place to rest his head.

Stars are up there and
out there some place.
He has seen them.

He remembers them
the same way that
they remember him.

They question his heat
and make pledges to
the circus of his bones.

adam releases the seas

Poison doesn't disappear.
Patient, it sits there
until every soul is yield.
Waits through all of
adam's generations
like it was fast-forwarding
through a commercial break.

Long before the Romans
carved every face in marble
to look only like Romans,
a cold-blooded serpent
saw safety in the trees.

Long before hallelujah
ever rolled around,
a sound bounced off
the canyon walls so hard
that seas collapsed
into a series of waves
that – to this day -
have not stopped.

serpent announces the third birth of adam

Every family tree is gigantic in the dark and his deceased
are warriors, still.
They have dispatched themselves to fetch each daybreak,
to set it at his feet

and never tire. At first, he doesn't notice the ghosts in his
periphery,
but he gradually reacquaints himself with faces and
forgotten voices;

cocks his head and steps nearer. They remind him of their
ancient warmth. He barely
takes note when he becomes one of them. Darkness brings
a different predator.

He starts to fetch daylight because they taught him to do so.
This is the unassuming recruitment program where adam
was born.

adam stays behind

adam was the one
who stayed behind
when the final snows
began to disappear
our cold browned world.

Green was muscle memory,
green was slow applause,
green was mere justification.

Green was slower and slower realization.

adam was the one
who stayed behind
when the tiny bones of spring
seemed as ancient
as stone upon dry stone.

adam discovers more than internal organs
during tenth grade biology class

Formaldehyde
cloud hovered
above adam's
raw teenage incision
into pickled skin,
thanks to his
clumsy hand upon
a sharp scalpel.
Too deep a first cut,
and at a thick,
awkward angle;
through stomach
and liver,
or what might
have been spleen.
There would be
no second cut.
There would be
no recovery
from his garish
entry wound.

adam defies both castor and pollux and walks
the beach at night

He took the sand
in his sheets as notice.
The poem was not how
waves broke on the rocks
when he stood there,
ankle deep in sand.
The poem was in the climb
down to the rocks
when the fine grains
settled between flesh
and footwear and
nobody was watching,
not even the twin brothers
roiling unwieldy
through the heavens.

eve sings to their offspring, song seven

daughters and sons
do not be a friend to the dollar sign/do not either make it an
enemy/know that it can be/both a bludgeon and a scalpel/
depending only upon who it is doing the wielding/remember
every maiden name on your mother's side/remember how
your father died

adam enlists forensics to investigate trace
evidence

Firing pin has left
its unique indentation
in the thickness
of adam's wounded
and thankful spine.
Casings are magnified;
set side-by-side on a
big screen in high definition
for a more complete analysis.
Ballistics seem to reveal
a closer and closer match.
The things he was and
the things he is are
converging upon exit
wounds not yet opened.

adam disregards the oceans

Tonight he sheds a tear
for the ocean floor, which
he has taken for granted,
expecting that it will be
there forever, a security
blanket that he'll not need.
Salted water rudely shouts
his name into the rocks,
warning the sand, just
before crashing down
like the misbegotten
sons of geronimo.

adam hides beneath the birchbark

He knows this ache
in his knees is temporary,
and will eventually allow for a
freer and straighter spine.
This is what he whispers
to himself, huddled under
the ribbed arch of an old canoe
his mother prepared for him
during the long last year
of absent sundowns, while
hoping he will remember
to stay upwind of predators.
She lamented the long, golden
horizon, knowing safety
would crinkle beneath adam
as he tried to tame his tremble.

eve sings to their offspring, song eight

daughters and sons
civilized life has made progress/we no longer believe that we
lose fundamental pieces of/our wretched souls simply from
having our photograph taken/   we are now owned by
phones/which unlock upon our eager garish faces/yours has
never been a world without electronics/without GPS/without
camera lenses pointing at you and from you/having never not
known this captivity/excavation is grey but necessary/you are
the only ones who can dig yourselves out from/underneath
bones you will never know

adam, however, fails to appreciate the threat

Lock inherently
understands that

not
every
damn
thing

needs to see
the light of day.

Secrets are secret
for a reason.

adam investigates the appeal of permanence

He knows this
requires both an
abundance of spirit
and a willingness
to subjugate himself
in the short-term,
knowing that
the construct
may – just may –
outlive the constructor.
His creation
may breathe on
in the dovetail joint
or in the word choice.
His voice will slowly
crawl on
in a technology
unimagined
by the temporary
absurdity of flesh.

adam develops a tactile cruelty and a discerning
eye for negative space

wide enough to see
all the beautiful teeth
in the mouth of the nile,
wide enough to unleash
color upon absence of color
and then add another shade
and another just to be safe,
wide enough to acknowledge
saints were sinners who
used to rely upon smoke
to fill our young lungs
when prayers sounded
like forgeries upon
our clumsy lips.

eve sings to their offspring, song nine

daughters and sons
regardless of your religion/sin at its core is an overwhelming
failure/to love/the closest human to you/the closest skin to
you/is not the only skin in the game/love the next one too/
and one after that

adam convinces himself the sextant
is a useful tool

adam listens to his rattling knees
and scapulae in the rotting wind.
He prays that he can find his pack,
so he doesn't have to fend for himself.
He understands that this will put
the grocery stores and the bars out of
business. He and the pack will run
from the churches with glorious abandon.
They will prey upon the north star
like they'll never need it again.

adam heads west because that is where the sun is

At first, it sounds like
the neighbor's dog howling
at sirens at early dusk,
so it's easy to dismiss.

Then the sirens disappear,
daylight is just about gone,
and the howl still sits,
ringing in his ears.

Closing all the windows
in the house doesn't silence
the howl, so he gets in his car
and turns on the radio.

adam measures his corner of the world

Bruises and backpedals
won't uncoil untruths,

So adam holds his hands up
in the shape of mountains;

in the shape of the flowers
he values the most: lily,
hydrangea, snapdragon;

in the shape of nineteen
hundred and eighty-one;

he holds his hands up
in the shape of a tomb;

in the shape of the heavens
he values the most:
bridge, electricity, mercy,
money, pain, open road;

serpent is in the world
now and adam knows
how knowledge tastes.
Coming clean is the only
way to save the skin.

serpent announces the fourth birth of adam

Rainwater ends every one of its busy days
soaking deep into the crooked dirt,

like ghosts in the periphery,
never once forgetting the science

behind the lift and the fall. All the while,
morning sits idly by, smelling of earthworms

and green grass and fruit that refuses to ripen.
This is the condensation where adam was born.

adam unearths a lost sermon

"with the steeple,
with the chase…"
This is all that remains
on his dusty clipboard
from the lost sermon,
from the rant sermon
that wrangled him from
birth to lacquered casket.
This is all that remains
from the undercurrents
of regret, of forced amnesia,
of being distracted by
all the shiny things in
all their brilliant packages.
This is all that remains
from the e-mail message
that says heart surgery,
that says high school
was two generations ago,
that says treat yourself
kindly because the
world has forgotten how.

adam watches the sea levels rise

Most to least, rivers roll over and through,
a small surrender to leaves on the trees.
Everything below water level is a murmur,

is the sound of melting ice. Kettles and keys
emerge as the new church bells, leaving
all remaining metals yellowish and weak.

This is not the last of the reforestation, of the
rejection of electric light, cauterizing the edge
of blue until death looks away, ecstatic.

adam loiters at the corner of blank page
and enter key

He stands around
until well after
sundown and
reminisces about
how things didn't
used to be like this.
And now his father
is a tombstone.
His mother is open wide;
she is the ghost of the buffalo,
the allegiance and the flag,
the ends that never meet,
the cobble-stoned streets,
the tempered steel,
the drowning pool,
the stained glass window,
a whispered prayer.

eve sings to their offspring, song ten

daughters and sons
there are very few things in the world more troubling/than
extended silences/you should not let yourself become one/
your heart is as big as you need it to be/remember how
your skin zippers against the skin of your lover/closes dark
space between you/turns it into almost light

adam races poison through eternity

Poison doesn't disappear.
That's the funny thing.

adam knows this permanence.
Patient, poison sits there

until every soul is yield;
waits through generations

like it was fast-forwarding
through a commercial break.

adam remembers the
unbending monochrome

strength of the serpent and
the weakened teeth & bones

of your father's mother
and your mother's father.

adam contemplates happenstance

adam knows
the gallop

comes for
each of our

hearts. He
knows some

will call
out in vain,

thinking a
small leap

in octave
will buy

one more
day or two.

adam says a tiny prayer of gratitude

Moss will eventually
get its hands on her.

adam knows this.
But not tonight, and
for this adam takes

his cue from George
Harrison's guitar.

eve sings to their offspring, song eleven

daughters and sons
cloud circles of crows will appear without notice sometimes/
show an applicable degree of awe/even though this black mass
will never know who you are/the face of god is not and never
will be/kaleidoscope or cotton white beard

adam forgets that his blood is an ocean

adam also forgets
that every breath is
a lesson in optimism,

that there is very little
difference between
inhale/exhale and

having one foot on
solid ground and the
other in the grave.

adam confronts himself in the dark

No awake like
two a.m. awake.
Eyes stay open,
everything is
digital green.
There is a noise
outside, something
mechanical;
it is not a
natural noise.
adam convinces
himself he has
no need to know
what it is.
Identifying it
as man-made
suffices tonight.

adam names the stillnesses

He sings himself to sleep,
counting stitches
upon his healing skin.
He sings himself to sleep,
avoiding the silence
between his previous
breath and what might be
his last breath.
He sings himself to sleep,
naming every stillness
in his family tree.
He sings himself to sleep,
knowing mountains and
the treacherous sun
collaborate to help
him join his dead.

eve sings to their offspring, song twelve

daughters and sons
glass can be as sharp as a knife/but it was sand or stone once/
once upon a time/is no way to be 20 one day and 50 the
next/nineteen hundred and ninety-five/is a quarter century
rearviewed already/ocean has never once/in that time/stopped
pulverizing the jagged shore

adam meekly explains games of chance

We won't know
who has the short straw
until it's too late,
until the heat subsides,
until we can't
push the tepid air
in and out
of our lungs any more
and only one of us
is left standing.
We won't know
who has the short straw
until all the money is counted,
until all of the wings are
neatly tucked along the backs of angels,
until the asphalt has cooled
and all our rambunctious children
can cross the streets barefoot.
We won't know
who has the short straw
until well after you and I
are gone and this building
we are sitting in
has burned and only
the walls are left,
covered in ivy.

adam counts out loud to twelve hundred

Breathing was easy
for adam, until it wasn't.
One morning, he woke up
and realized his earthly world
had become a vise.
Floorboards were a jaw and
roof was a jaw and
both were tightening the life
from him. He crawled inside
the safety of his own rib cage,
poked holes in his lungs
so he would not suffocate.
He let the nail of his pinkie finger
grow jagged and scratched
a single line into his pleura
as each day passed.
One became two
became three became four
became twelve hundred
until there was no more
unscratched surface.
Every square inch was perforation.
And just like that,
there was no more counting
to be done.

adam unbuilds a box

He identifies and attacks
         any and all nail holes.
He unscrews and removes
the hinged lid from box.
He removes the sides
         of the box from the base.
He unassembles the butt joints.
He uncuts his boards.
He unmeasures and
         unmarks his boards.
He ignores his supplies.
He returns wood into tree forms.
He leaves the trees alone.
He plants one more,
         just to be safe.
adam remembers blue sky.

serpent announces the final birth of adam

Past, present, and future are all visible at once.
They align with the sun this time of year,

scald their dislocation into ugly remnants upon
the earth, soaking deep into the crooked dirt.

Muscle and bone disentangle into a
bouquet of days wilting around him.

Past, present, and future are all visible at once.
This is the triptych where adam was born.

Steve Brightman lives in Akron, OH with his wife and their green parrot, who rules the roost. Brightman's last full length collection is titled *The Wild Gospel of Careening and Other Sermons from the Rumble Strip*" (Red Orchid Press).

BLACK DRAGON POETRY SOCIETY

CERTIFIED AND APPROVED